by

Produced by
MEF English

www.mefworld.com

ISBN: 978-1-7387992-5-1

KEYWORDS

rabbit

beach

pig

swimsuits

monkey

beach balls

hot

beach umbrella

Once there were 3 friends.

The first one was a rabbit .

“I am a rabbit ,” said rabbit .

I am a rabbit.

The second one was a pig.

"I am a pig," said pig.

I am a pig.

The third one was a monkey.

"I am a monkey," said monkey.

I am a monkey.

The day was very hot.

They wanted to go to the beach.

“Let’s go to the 

!”

said 

.

“What should we take

to the 

?”

asked 

.

Let's go to the Beach!

"We need swimsuits,"

said rabbit.

"How many swimsuits?"

asked pig.

"Three," said rabbit.

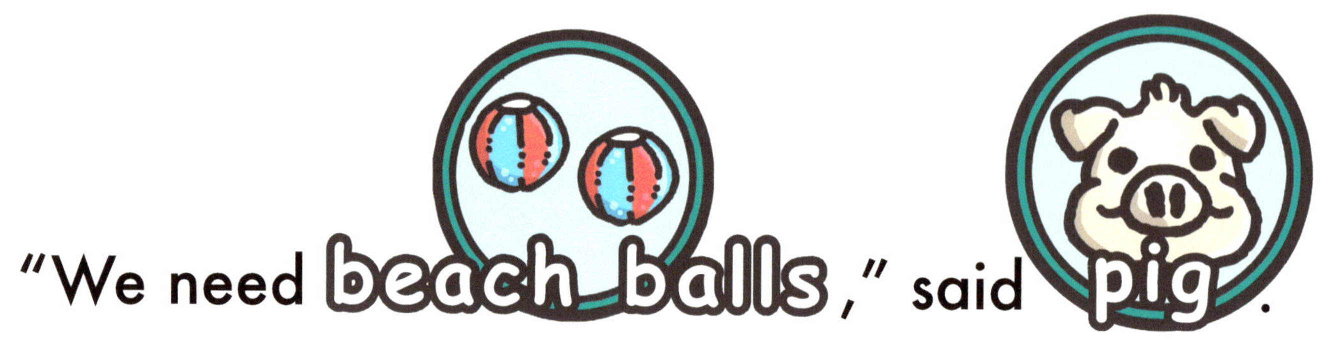

"We need beach balls," said pig.

"How many beach balls?"

asked monkey.

"Two," said pig.

"We need a beach umbrella,"

said monkey.

"How many umbrellas?" asked rabbit .

"One," said monkey.

Rabbit got the swimsuits .

"I have three swimsuits ,"

said rabbit .

I have 3 swimsuits.

Pig got the beach balls.

"I have two beach balls,"

said pig.

I have 2 beach balls.

Monkey got the beach umbrella.

"I have one beach umbrella,"

said monkey.

I have 1 beach umbrella.

So, rabbit, pig and monkey went to the beach on the hot day.

They swam in the water,

played with the beach balls,

and played under the beach umbrella.

The friends had fun at the beach.

The
END

Trace the letters, practice writing.

rabbit

pig

monkey

beach

Find and color the beach things.

Find and circle 5 differences between the pictures.

Let's
go to the
Beach!

www.mefworld.com

Free Bonus Content

Watch the Animated Version

Guarantee

MEF English guarantees our books. If you have any issue at all, please contact

info@mefworld.com

Children's Books by MEF English

Visit Amazon, search

"MEF English"

for the following books:

- Our Colorful Painting
- Potatoes are Vegetables
- The Snake and the Rabbit
- The Fire Fighter the Pilot and the Doctor
- Dolphin's Dream
- The Soccer Game
- A Bug Tea Party
- Happy Feelings
- Emma's Christmas
- 4 People in my Family
- Suzy's Valentine's Day
- Monsters Have Feelings Too!
- Let's go to the Beach
- Little Jellyfish

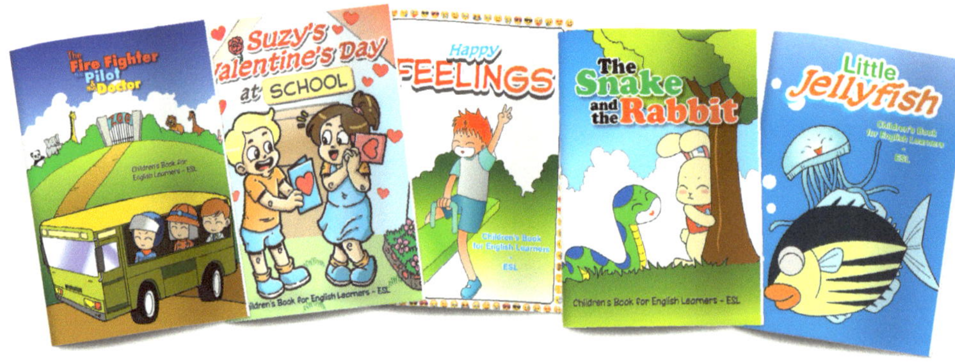

Business / Travel
Book by CEO
of MEF English
Derek J. Keet

Thank you for reading!

Let's go to the Beach!

Review

The amount of effort that MEF teachers put into the MEF English materials for the education of young children should not go unnoticed. If you are able to help promote our materials with a review we will greatly appreciate it.

For reviews on other countries, please kindly find the book page and click on the review link.

Visit

mefworld.com

for more educational materials

www.ingramcontent.com/pod-product-compliance
Ingram Content Group UK Ltd.
Pitfield, Milton Keynes, MK11 3LW, UK
UKHW060122300726
14090UKWH00002B/307

* 9 7 8 1 7 3 8 7 9 9 2 5 1 *